Meditation and the Art of Writing

Meditation and the Art of Writing

Learn to control your brain-waves, unlock your
creative muse, and conquer writer's block forever!

By Chad Kunego

What The...?!? Publishing

Copyright/Disclaimer

Editing, cover and interior layout by Chad Kunego
Printed in the United States of America

ChadKunego@gmail.com

What the...?!? Publishing
131 W. Seneca St. #109
Manlius, NY 13104

Dedication and acknowledgements

I dedicate this book to my wife, Heather. Without her understanding, this book might not have ever happened. She let me wander up to my office, a.k.a. my writer's Man Cave instead of spending more time with her after work or when I'd stay up until 8am writing or researching something and then sleep until the late afternoon on my days off. Love you more. "That's my baby!"

I also would like to say thanks to Emily A. for being my beta reader and test subject. Your input improved this book and gave me confidence that I was on the right track. Thanks for the use of your brain, since I seem to have misplaced mine.

Contents

Forward 11

Introduction 13

Chapter 1 15
  Writer's Block 15

Chapter 2 19
  Benefits of regular meditation 19
  Quiets your mind and body 20
  Helps you put aside your daily concerns 22
  Lowers your stress level 23
  Provides you a mental space to allow ideas to form 24
  Unlocks creativity and helps quiet the logical/inner
  critic part of your mind 25
  Helps synchronize both sides of the brain 26

Chapter 3 29
  Next stop: The brain-wave patterns/levels 29
    What are brain-wave levels? 30
      Beta brain-wave pattern - Where most people
      normally function 31
      Alpha brain-Wave pattern - Where the magic starts ... 31
      Theta brain-wave pattern - You are getting sleepy 33
      Delta brain-wave pattern 33
      Gamma brain-wave pattern 34
  So what? 35
  What levels are best/worst for writing? 35

Chapter 4   **37**
  Types of meditation   37
    Internal/External   40
    Guided/Unguided   42
    Verbal/Nonverbal   43
    Moving/Stationary   44
  Time commitment   46

Chapter 5   **47**
  Technology   47
  Pros/Cons of using technology   47
  Types of technology   48
    Aural   49
     Binaural beats   50
      HemiSync   51
      Holosync   52
      Paraliminal   52
     Isochronic beats   54
      The Unexplainable Store   55
    Visual   56
    Kinesthetic   57
  Use before or during writing   57

Chapter 6   **59**
  A few sample styles of meditation   59
    The Silva Method - A brief overview   61
    4-count meditation   63
    Walking/Running meditation   64
    Other forms to pursue   65

Chapter 7	**67**
Odds and Ends	67
Eye position	67
Mind Mapping	69
Image streaming	70
"Putting on Heads"	72
The habit of writing every day	73
5-point essay	74
Diet/Nutrition	77
Chapter 8	**81**
In Closing	81
Before you go...	82
Appendix A	**85**
My experience with meditation and reduced amount of sleep	85
Appendix B	**87**
Bibliography/References/Further reading	**87**
Notes	**88**

FORWARD

Back many, many moons ago, I remember sitting in class, trying to figure out how to write an essay. I had great ideas, but when I put pen to paper, they all seemed to vanish, only to leave ghostly remnants behind, almost mocking me. At the time, I couldn't understand why. I'd had child psychologists tell my parents that I had some type of learning disability in connection to my hyperactivity, but all that mumbo-jumbo didn't help one bit when it came time to write.

Thankfully, one of my teachers had the brilliant idea of having me try to write on one of those newfangled devices they just got in the classroom called an Apple II computer. Because I had spent hours upon hours copying and typing in program listings out of magazines at home, using a computer was a very familiar and comfortable process for me.

Once seated at the computer, the words suddenly flew from my mind to my fingers faster than I could touch type. It wasn't a fluke, either. From that point forward, whenever I had to write something, I was allowed to use the computer to do it.

Looking back on it, I wondered how I was suddenly able to go from not being able to put one full sentence down to being able to write short stories almost instantly. What changed between struggling to try and lay down one word with pen and paper to having the words just gush out of me while at a computer?

I realize now that what I had was a severe case of writer's block when I was in high school. So the question then became, how did I go from having a severe case of writer's block to being totally creative just because I switched from using a pen and paper to using a keyboard? Was it just a case of using a different tool to write with, or was there something more going on behind the scenes?

For the next 25 years, I've delved into accelerative learning, speed-reading and speed-learning, meditation, Neuro-Linguistic Programming, and numerous other technologies trying to answer that question, along with trying to prove to myself and others that I was capable of doing much more with my life than what my school guidance counselor said was the best career for me… A photographer's assistant.

It also allowed me to overcome my 'learning disabilities' by discovering how I learned best and learned how to cope with the symptoms of hyperactivity, or using the more politically correct term, Attention Deficit Hyperactive Disorder. It also led me to realize what writer's block actually is and how to overcome it easily.

Letting a friend beta read this book allowed them to improve their ability to organize their information and noticeably improve their writing speed for college papers. I hope that it'll do the same for you as well. I hope you enjoy the journey you're about to begin as much as I enjoyed sharing the map with you.

Chad Kunego

January 2, 2014

INTRODUCTION

Writer's block… The bane of a writer's existence. Once it shows up, it seems like it's almost impossible to get past. On the flip side, you love the days where you sit down to write, the ideas start flowing, and the next think you know, it's 3 hours later and you've written over 3,000 words of really good stuff.

What most writers don't realize is that they're both sides of the same coin. What's even better, and somewhat surprising for anyone who's ever experienced writer's block, is that you have a lot of control over which side of the coin happens to be facing up. Some of it obviously has to do with your attitude, your outlook on life, and your confidence level, but some of it has to do with the way your brain is actually running at the time.

One of the best ways to change the way your brain is operating is through some form of meditation. Most of the books I've read on writing touched on the concept, but didn't actually name it meditating. For example, three of the five steps mentioned by Dene Low in her book, <u>Write Like Your Brain Works</u>, can easily be construed as a form of meditation, things like: maintaining that hazy, half-awake/half asleep state you're in when you first start to wake up or doing some type of movement activity where you're in motion but doesn't require a lot of thought, like running, swimming, or walking.

You might think it's a mystery why doing stuff like this help break through writer's block and open the floodgate of ideas, but other actions don't. There's actually no mystery why once you understand how your brain functions.

So, keep an open mind and a notebook handy, and hopefully by the end, you'll never fear suffering from writer's block again.

CHAPTER 1

WRITER'S BLOCK

In all the world of writing, nothing seems to strike fear into the heart of a writer more than the blank page. More specifically, a page that remains blank. Writer's block has probably destroyed the creation of more worlds, characters, and the advancement of science and understanding than any other reason.

Yes, I'm being overly dramatic to an extent, but if you think about it, there's more truth to it than you'd expect. Think about all the stories, in all the different genres, that never get told; the people in those untold fantastic worlds who never come alive, and all the scientific discoveries that never get shared with the public because the author couldn't get past that blank page.

When someone sits down to write a story, they usually have a bunch of ideas they'd like to share. Once they sit down and stare at that blank page, the ability to find the right words seems to vanish. Or maybe they've already got part of what they want to tell written down, but all of a sudden, it comes to a screeching halt. They've hit the proverbial dry well when they try and figure out how to continue their story.

What most writers don't realize is that this is the beginning of an internal feedback loop that, if not addressed quickly, will usually spiral out of control to the point where they can't go any further. The sad thing is, in this age of technology and wealth of knowledge available, most authors don't realize that there's a whole slew of tools available to help them break the cycle and get back on track.

One of the best tools available to authors in general, and blocked ones in particular, is meditation. In and of itself, it has quite a few beneficial effects that can help a writer be more creative and productive. Once you know what's going on behind the scenes when you meditate, however, you'll realize there's more ways to help get past any writer's block issues you have.

Along the way, you'll learn that there's a whole world of different forms of meditation: from stationary ones, moving ones, ones where you chant, and ones where you're silent. The reason why I bring this up is that, since everyone is different, a meditation style that works for one person may not work for another.

One of the big things that's going to be covered is your brain-wave states and how they can affect you and your writing. Once you understand the different brain-wave levels, you'll begin to see what you're actually accomplishing when you meditate and why it helps you with your writing sometimes but not others.

Me personally, depending on my mood, I sometimes like a standing type of meditation that's internally focused, no verbal components, and some upper body movement. At other times, I've used guided meditation, in a seated position, to try and work through a specific issue.

The point is, if all you thought you did for meditation was sit on a pillow with your legs crossed going "OM" for hours on end, then you might be in for a pleasant surprise. With all the different forms of meditation out there, there's bound to be a style that matches your personality and temperament; one that's going to be of great help to you on your path as a writer.

The type of meditation you eventually choose isn't as important as what happens inside your brain when you find the one that works for you. It's only after you find the one that helps you reach the brain-wave states of Alpha and Theta that you'll be able to say goodbye to writer's block forever.

In the next chapter, I'm going to go over some of the general benefits that any form of meditation provides. These benefits alone might be enough to help you get through a mild case of writer's block. Even better, you'll start thinking more clearly because you'll be learning how to focus your thoughts more easily. With that in mind, let's begin.

CHAPTER 2

BENEFITS OF REGULAR MEDITATION

In and of itself, meditation has a long list of health benefits, both physical and mental. Just a small list includes:

- Better mental clarity

- Lower stress levels

- Lower blood pressure

- Ability to concentrate longer

- Greater awareness of your environment

- Deep relaxation

- Increased mental alertness

- Lowered heart and respiration rates

- Decreases in blood-lactate levels (higher levels are attributed
  to stress, tension, and anxiety)

Even with this abbreviated list, it would be hard to argue against the idea that meditation would be of significant benefit to anyone who practiced it. It would be even harder to say that most of these benefits wouldn't greatly help a writer in particular.

Assuming you're a professional writer, being able to relax and release tension allows you to work more efficiently when you have a deadline to meet instead of stressing over it. Being able to block out that deadline and concentrate for extended periods of time on your writing alone gives you a much better chance of meeting or even beating that deadline.

Improving your mental clarity means you'd be able to craft a more concise passage or more convincing argument, without needing some form of stimulant, like caffeine. Increased mental alertness might also mean noticing more details in your environment, details that might spark your creativity, helping you generate the next blockbuster.

It goes without saying how having a slower heart rate and lower blood pressure would benefit someone. Same thing with reducing their blood-lactate levels. Some of the biggest health issues today are caused by increased stress and anxiety. Having an all-natural, non-pharmaceutical way to help with those issues is a big bonus.

Now obviously I'm not a doctor, nor do I play one on TV, so it goes without saying that you need to check with your own doctor to see if it's possibly for you to address these health risks without medication, or maybe even just a reduced dosage over what you might be taking now.

Quiets your mind and body

The biggest benefit, at least in my opinion, regular meditation sessions can do for a writer is to quiet both your mind and body, improving the functioning of both. Just as physical exercise can improve your endurance and strength levels, regular meditation can help improve your brain/mind functioning and the efficiency of your heart and lungs.

While cardiovascular exercises, like aerobics, help your heart and lungs by making them stronger and more efficient (through adaptive things like a larger heart that pumps more blood per beat, or better transport of oxygen to the bloodstream via better lung function), meditation does it in a different manner.

During most forms of meditation, your stress levels tend to decrease sharply. With lower stress levels, you tend to take deeper inhalations. For some forms of meditation, you even focus specifically on breathing lower into your lungs.

It's my belief that, with these deeper levels of relaxation and higher levels of oxygen being available in the bloodstream, your heart doesn't have to work as hard. This reduction in workload allows the heart to relax a little, which in turn allows it to slow down its rate of pumping. Beating more slowly reduces the oxygen requirement of the body, which allows the body to slow respiration, which again lowers the oxygen requirement.

Granted, these are just some of the reasons for the lowered heart and respiration rate. Science isn't really sure of all the reasons for the decrease in rate. There's some speculation that meditation activates the parasympathetic nervous system. Irrespective of the whys behind it, regular meditative practice has been scientifically shown to cause slower breathing, lowered heart rate, deepening relaxation levels, and lower stress levels.

Another possible benefit is a reduced need for sleep. A lot of the evidence it anecdotal, but if you're interested, I relate my own experience with significantly reduced amounts of sleep while still being able to function. My personal account is in Appendix A.

Through regular meditation practice, if you had the ability to get up an hour or two earlier every day just to write while still feeling just as rested as if you got a full night's sleep, how much more productive would you be? In other words, right at the top of the list of excuses most people have for not writing is lack of time. Through regular meditation, you're eliminated that excuse. If you got up an hour earlier and meditated for 15-30 minutes, it'd still leave you 30-45 minutes to write. What's even better, and for reasons I'm going to cover in the next chapter, you'd even be more productive and creative by meditating first, before you wrote, than if you tried to start writing immediately. You might even be able to accomplish more in that 30-45 minutes after a meditation session than you might be able to do with a dedicated 1-2 hours of writing without meditation.

Helps you put aside your daily concerns

This leads right into my next point. Assuming you can't write when you first get up in the morning, it's sometimes hard to sit down and start writing later in the day because you've got a million things running through your mind. Whether it's thinking about doing the grocery shopping, needing to do a load of laundry, taking the kids to some type of practice event, or thinking about what you're going to have for dinner, trying to get focused on writing can seem nearly impossible.

If you start your writing sessions with just 10-15 minutes worth of meditation, or even just 5 minutes if that's all you can spare, you can gently clear your mind and set aside all your concerns for the day. Once that's done, you'll be able to more easily focus on the writing task at hand.

The ability to clear your mind is a well-documented benefit when it comes to meditation. In the beginning, you might not be too successful at it, but with practice, time, and experience, it'll become second nature to you.

Being able to approach your writing sessions with a clear mind can't be overstated. It's hard to think of how your hero is going to escape from their exploding spaceship if you're still thinking about that water bill you still need to pay. It'll still be there later whether you've written anything or not, but not having to think about it while writing will make a huge difference in your productivity and creativity levels.

Lowers your stress level

Another thing that's a bane of every writer is stress. When you're stressed out, it's hard to be creative. There's some very real physiological reasons for impaired creativity while being stressed, which I'll talk more about in the next chapter. You probably don't need me to tell you that trying to write while being stressed feels similar to hiking through knee-high mud… tiring and you don't get very far.

With just a brief meditation session, especially the more physical types like Tai-Chi, you'll have the opportunity to work out some of that stress without becoming exhausted, like you might be by going to the gym and working out. It also doesn't require any special equipment to meditate, unlike most forms of exercise you might do at the gym.

I'm not trying to imply that you'll never need to go to the gym if you meditate regularly. Far from it. Getting regular exercise can do wonders for your energy levels, your cognitive abilities due to improved oxygen use and cardiovascular fitness, and your overall ability to actually deal with stress physically.

What I'm saying is, when you don't have time to go to the gym, a short session of a more physical type of meditation might suffice. Once you've blown off some steam, you'll be more energized and ready to sit down and pound away at your keyboard for a while.

Provides you a mental space to allow ideas to form

What all this really means is, by getting in the habit of meditating on a regular basis, you develop the ability to clear out a mental space in your mind for ideas to form. It's like sitting down at your desk at work and tidying up before you start on a project. If your desk is in complete shambles when you sit down, it's going to be more difficult to work. You're going to be shuffling papers, moving stuff, and just puttering around instead of focusing on the task at hand.

Meditation does the same thing for your *inner* workspace. By gently clearing out an area to work and organizing everything beforehand, you allow the ideas to start flowing into that space you created. The more consistently you practice, and the longer you pursue it, the larger that space becomes. Over time, that space will become less cluttered between sessions, meaning it'll take less "work" to clear it the next time. It also means that, as you go through your day, you'll have a space to put things. In other words, as you progress with your practice, you'll become more observant of the world around you. Your environment will take on more vibrancy and will have a richer texture than what you've been used to in the past.

This new "life" will bring forth new ideas and you'll begin to notice more things that you might have ignored in the past. I have this happen all the time. I get fascinated by things around me that most people will never become aware of. For example, I might be walking around in my yard and notice an ant struggling with a piece of a leaf. I might wind up observing that ant for 10 minutes, wondering what that ant might be experiencing while it struggles to bring that little morsel back to its home.

My wife is always surprised when I can spot wildlife hiding on the side of the road while we're driving. I don't try to spot it, but because of my heightened level of awareness, they just stick out to me.

I can't say with 100% certainty that it's just from my many years of meditation practice, but I know that if I had never meditated, I doubt I'd be as observant as I am today. As a side note, this observational ability doesn't seem to extend to things that need to be done around the house. Go figure...

Unlocks creativity and helps quiet the logical/inner critic part of your mind

Once you get used to creating this mental space, your level of creativity should start to improve. It might not be very noticeable, at least in the beginning, but over time you'll be able to develop more and better ideas to work with and write about. When you're meditating, by necessity and as a physiological function of going into an alpha brain-wave pattern that I'll talk about later, you learn to turn of the logical side of your mind. I'm not saying you become dumb, but the urge to figure out and rationalize everything takes on less importance.

As the left brain/logical side of your mind quiets down, your right brain/creative side becomes more active. Now to be clear, your whole brain isn't physically divided in half. Science has basically disproved that myth. That being said, there is a part of the brain, the neocortex to be exact, that is basically divided into the left/logical and right/creative side of the brain.

For our purpose here, it's just an easier way to explain what happens during meditation. The part of the neocortex that deals with logical thought processes quiets down and the creative side gets more active. What this means for you is, by regularly meditating, you'll have greater access to the creative centers of your mind.

Helps synchronize both sides of the brain

An important point to keep in mind is that, while it is significantly muted, the logical side of your mind isn't completely turned off while meditating. If it was, you'd be amazingly creative, but you wouldn't be able to write because the left side of the mind controls language. If you were an artist, you might rely almost entirely on your right/creative side while creating your art, but you wouldn't be able to verbally articulate it very well.

In order to write well, you need access to both "sides" of the brain. Through regular meditative practice, you'll start developing those stronger pathways between both hemispheres. With some forms of meditation, and/or some technological help, both sides become synchronized and function at a higher level than either side can do independently.

This phenomena is called whole mind thinking. One of the tools I'll cover later makes great use of this phenomena. A company that created some wonderful tools to create this effect is called Learning Strategies, who I'll also talk about later. Their series of Paraliminal® recordings makes great use of activating your whole mind through several different technologies.

With whole mind thinking, you'll be able to more easily come up with great ideas, be able to write faster than you currently do (unless you're writing as fast as you can physically type/write/talk into a recorder), and be more relaxed while writing. This synchronization will impact other areas of your life for the better as well. You'll be able to express ideas more clearly, your memory will usually improve, your problem solving ability will get better, and you'll be able to handle stress better. In other words, you'll start functioning at a higher level than you are now. Over time, people WILL start to notice the change.

With that said, let's move on to what's actually happening in the brain when you meditate.

CHAPTER 3

NEXT STOP: THE BRAIN-WAVE PATTERNS/LEVELS

In the previous chapter, I went over some of the benefits of meditation and how it can help with your writing. In this chapter, I'm going to go over the how and why it provides these benefits. At the same time, once you understand what's going on behind the scenes when you're meditating, you'll be able to figure out what methods and processes will help you the most to break through writer's block.

Throughout this book, I'll pretty much use the terms level, pattern, and state interchangeably, although they mean slightly different things. With that said, the biggest thing to understand is the different brain-wave patterns your brain operates at. Learning the different patterns and what happens at each level will propel you on your way to being a more creative writer and help banish writer's block from ever darkening your doorstep again.

Unfortunately, this information is going to be a bit on the dry and technical side. If you really wanted to, you could skip to the next chapter if you'd like. You'd still get all the benefits I've mentioned without ever reading it. However, if you really want to know what's going on behind the curtain of your mind, where your muse frolics, then you'll want to come back and read this material at some point.

What are brain-wave levels?

First off, what you need to understand is that every moment that you're alive and kicking, your brain is functioning at different frequency levels. These levels or patterns are easily recognizable when monitored on a device called an Electroencephalograph, or EEG machine. They're those devices you see in the movies where the doctor hooks wires up to the patient's head and looks at a readout, usually to determine if the patient is brain dead or not. Their readings are displaying what frequencies your brain is operating at, measured in Hertz (Hz).

Understanding what Hertz and cycles per second mean plays a very important role in the rest of this discussion, so it's imperative that you understand what it means. To start with, 1Hz = 1 cycle per second. One cycle is going from zero, progressing to the highest point in the cycle (peak), dropping back down to zero, progressing to the lowest point in the cycle (peak), and then progressing back up to zero.

A good way to visualize it is by thinking about taking a length of rope, tying one end to a stationary object, and shaking in up and down in a steady rhythmic manner. The waves that form have a top and a bottom. Each complete wave from neutral, to top, back to neutral, to bottom, and back neutral again is a complete cycle.

Also, although they mean slightly different things, for simplicity, I'll be using the words pattern, rhythm, frequency, and state interchangeably during the following discussion.

Beta brain-wave pattern - Where most people normally function

When you're wide awake and conscious, even though you generate patterns from all four categories all the time, if you're like most people, you're primarily operating in a Beta brain-wave pattern. These patterns start at 13Hz and go up from there.

At 13Hz and working up to 30Hz, you become more focused, have a higher level of concentration, and are more alert. Above 30 Hz, you experience uneasiness, distress, and anxiety[1], at least for Beta brain-wave patterns. Gamma brain-wave patterns overlap Beta waves and are talked about a little later in this section.

The higher range of beta frequency patterns induce the fight or flight response. The reason all this is important is, the higher into the beta range you go, the farther away you get from the brain-wave categories that allows creativity. In other words, the more stress you generate, the less creative you're physiologically able to be because you're creeping up into higher beta brain-wave frequencies and further away from the frequency ranges conducive to creativity.

Alpha brain-Wave pattern - Where the magic starts

Alpha brain-wave patterns/rhythm occur between 8Hz-12.9Hz. This frequency level is usually reached when you're just drifting off to sleep or just waking up under normal circumstances, but can usually be induced during most forms of meditative practice. It's also the state you go into to some extent when you focus on something you're trying to learn or absorb, like reading a book.

---

1   Bill Harris, *Thresholds of the Mind*, pg 25

Scientists have known, since at least 1979, that certain groups of people — yogis with almost photographic memories, instant calculators, and people with heightened levels of creativity — when using their abilities, drop into an Alpha brain-wave rhythm.[2]

At the higher end of the Alpha frequency range, you go into what scientists have called a "super-learning" state. Absorbing information becomes much easier and you tend to remember it longer. It's also at this level that we start to become introspective.

Another benefit of this level is that it shuts off your inner critic. According to José Silva, author of the Silva Mind Control Method, you can't think negative thoughts at all while in the Alpha state.[3] If you try, you pop out of the Alpha brain-wave state.

What this means for you as a writer is that you're not going to be second guessing yourself while you're writing. The words will flow more smoothly and you won't keep going back to correct things while you're maintaining an Alpha brain-wave pattern.

Since you can't experience stress while in Alpha state — since stress is associated with Beta brain-wave patterns — your main source of writer's block disappears, allowing you to work more easily "in the zone".

This, by itself, might be all you need to unlock your creativity and allow your muse to run free across the page, but there's another, lower level of brain-wave pattern where your muse has their cozy little home set up and where you can visit them when you want, once you know how to do it.

---

2   Sheila Ostrander, Lynn Schroeder, Nancy Ostrander, *Super-learning* pg 63
3   José Silva, *The Silva Mind Control Method*, pg 29-30

Theta brain-wave pattern - You are getting sleepy

The next level of brain-waves is Theta. This level falls in the 4Hz-7.9Hz frequency range. Per Bill Harris, author of the book Thresholds of the Mind, "Theta is associated with enhanced creativity, memory, healing, and integrative experiences, where we put together previously disparate pieces of information, leading to an "ah-ha" experience.[4]"

The part I want to draw your attention to is the enhanced creativity part. Theta brain-wave patterns are also believed, by some people, to be the doorway to the unconscious mind.

The downside is, Theta is very difficult for the average person to reach reliably while remaining conscious. Most people only enter a strong Theta state when they're asleep. Even Zen monks have a hard time reaching that level of consciousness while remaining awake and aware of their surroundings.

Later in this book I'll talk about ways to bypass years of training to allow you to reach the Theta state almost at will, both before and during your writing period. And it won't require a forced retreat at your local monastery.

Delta brain-wave pattern

This level of brain wave functioning, 0.1Hz-3.9Hz, is the lowest and slowest brain wave frequency. In reference to writing, there's no real way or need to reach this level of consciousness. Granted, it's possible to reach using some of the methods mentioned later, getting to this level during writing won't be of any help.

---

4   Bill Harris, *Thresholds of the Mind*, pg 26

This level of brain-wave function is associated with dreamless sleep, so no real creativity happens at this level. There are some theoretical things that happen at this level that could possibly help with your creativity, like a possible window into the collective unconscious, but this is better accessed while sleeping.

During sleep, if you've loaded up your conscious thoughts with possible problems with your writing, your access to Delta (and other brain-wave frequency ranges) may help you find a solution. Until you've gained practice and experience doing this, your results may vary.

Gamma brain-wave pattern

This is the most recent brain-wave level discovered. There's not really a lot known about it, nor is there really any way to access it on command. There may eventually be a way to access it in the future, but the only reason I mention it here is just to be complete.

What little is known about this level is that it seems to overlap slightly with the Beta level. With Beta level, as previously noted, when you start to get above 30Hz, you tend to start developing more stress, among other things.

This is where it gets interesting. Gamma levels start at between 25Hz-30Hz and go up from there, to at least 100Hz. Initial findings are indicating that this level of brain-wave frequencies are connected to peak concentration and extremely high levels of cognitive functioning.[5]

---

5   http://www.omharmonics.com/blog/gamma-brain-waves/
      — 5th paragraph

This range is also starting to be associated to memory recall, at around 40Hz, and entering "the zone." Hopefully more research will become available over time since this frequency range may have a strong impact on your focus while writing.

So what?

So why does all this matter? If you're like most writers, you barely have enough time in the day to actually sit down and try to write, let alone setting aside time to meditate.

I hope this very brief overview gets you thinking about what would happen to your writing ability if you could, in fact, take advantage of what the different brain-wave states offer. The important thing to keep in mind is, what brain-wave state you're in when you sit down to write can have a very real impact on your ability to write. If you're running too high in the Beta range, you might not even be able to write creatively at all.

By learning to use a few relaxation exercises, meditative practices, and technological solutions, you'll know how to attack and overcome writer's block since you'll know some of the root causes for it.

What levels are best/worst for writing?

Another way to look at it is this: when you sit down to write, the closer you can get to Alpha/Theta, the easier it's going to be for you to write creatively. Conversely, the higher into Beta you get, the harder it's going to be write.

Now all this doesn't happen in a vacuum. As I mentioned previously, you have a mixture of all these states going on at any particular time. With practice, and possibly technology, you can function in Beta (so you remain conscious), but you'll also be able to increase your levels of Alpha and Theta patterns as well, granting you better access to the creative parts of your mind.

CHAPTER 4

TYPES OF MEDITATION

So now that you know some of the benefits of meditation and have an understanding of some of what's happening in the background, it's time to actually start talking about different types of meditation.

Most people, when asked what it means to meditate, believe it's sitting cross-legged in a Lotus position repeatedly saying OM over and over. Some of the more knowledgeable might also mention that Tai-Chi and Yoga are also forms of meditation as well.

What's surprising to most people, once they really start looking into it, is how many different forms of meditation are actually available. If you took a strict definition of what meditation is, prayer actually falls into this category.

So what is meditation really? The simplest definition is mindfully focusing on one thing to the exclusion of everything else. Or at least that's the goal. In the beginning, it might feel like an exercise in herding cats in a rainstorm, but over time, you begin to learn how to bring yourself back to your object of focus until one day you realize that you only had that one thing in your conscious awareness.

Unfortunately, that realization breaks you out of that "oneness" and you're back to square one. But with continued practice, those periods of "oneness" extend for longer and longer stretches of time.

Monks spend their entire life trying to get to the point where they can maintain that one-mind state at all times. I'm not suggesting you need to do that in order to be more creative and never again have writer's block. Far from it. What I am suggesting is that you'll eventually get to the point, while still having a normal life, of not stressing about getting writer's block. And if it ever does rear its ugly head, you'll have the tools needed to gently tell it to go away because you're busy.

Writer's block isn't something that you can banish by force of will. But as with any other distracting thoughts, you'll learn to see it, welcome it into your mind, acknowledge it, then put it aside so you can continue with your writing.

It almost sounds like an oxymoron that you'd want to welcome writer's block into your mind, but once you've reached a certain point on your meditative journey, you'll see it for what it is, *your mind trying to stop you from doing work*. Once you can acknowledge it, you'll be able to set it aside and get back to what you're doing.

It comes down to focus. If I told you to absolutely, positively, under no circumstance, think about a pink elephant, what's the first thing that pops in your head? A pink elephant. The more I tell you not to think about it, the harder it becomes to keep that image out of your head.

If I told you it was OK to think about that elephant, but from there, think about a flying dolphin, you'd probably just have a passing image of an elephant and then move on to that dolphin.

Why is that? It's because you welcomed that image of the pink elephant into your conscious thoughts, but you were able to move on because you weren't dwelling on it or focusing on trying to keep in out of your mind.

Writer's block is the same thing. The more you try and fight against and resist it, the firmer it's going to plant itself in your mind. By welcoming it and acknowledging it, you're giving yourself the needed space to be able to push it to the side and continue on with your writing. You go with the flow instead of fighting against it.

So without further ado, here's the different types of meditation you have to choose from. A lot of these are taken from a wonderful book on meditation called <u>How to Meditate</u> by Lawrence LeShan.

It's the first book on meditating I ever bought, back when I was around 16 years old, and I refer back to it on a semi-regular basis. For the styles of meditation that aren't referred to in this book, I'll provide the necessary reference when needed.

Another thing is that some forms of meditation may fall under more than one category, which I'll note as well. One final note to make is that all these different categories can be grouped together into three more general categories. These categories are:

- The path of Intellect

- The path of Emotion

- The path of Action

Another way to categorize all these type of meditations are whether they're structured or unstructured. A good way to think of this differentiation is whether you start the journey like someone with a road map, or are you like water flowing down a hill, following a random pattern that only makes sense after you've traveled it.

As I go through each category, it should become apparent which of these categories the different types of meditation fall under.

Internal/External

The first category of meditative practice deals with where your focus is, either internal or external. What I mean by this is whether you're focusing on something outside your body, like a mandala or maybe an interesting stone, or whether it's internal to you, like your heartbeat, your breathing, or maybe your stream of thought.

Since it's usually easier to start with, I'm going to discuss external forms of meditation first. The easiest form of this type of meditation deals with taking an ordinary object and focusing on it. This doesn't mean just look at it. It means really, and I mean really, observe it. Nor does it mean making a judgment about it, or trying to determine what it means to you. It means you're going to look at it like you would if you'd never seen it before.

Imagine you're an alien and have come to Earth for the first time. For this example, we'll use a very common object, a quarter. If you'd never seen one before and had no idea of its significance, what would you notice?

Would you notice its heft? Is it shiny or dull? Are you looking at the side with a head on it, or is it tail's side up? Is it warm to the touch or cool? How warm or cool? Compared to what? Your hand, the air, the surface you're sitting on? What does it feel like? Can you feel the ridges around the outside edge?

You get the idea. After looking at it, can you visualize it with your eyes closed? How close were you when you opened your eyes to observe it again? Did you miss that little nick on it?

That's it. Nothing more, nothing less. Your entire job is to really notice this item to the exclusion of all other thoughts. Once you feel that you really know this item, you can choose another item to focus on, but you normally wouldn't switch objects until after using the current object for several sessions.

With an internal focus, you're using the same powers of observation, but turned inward. If you're using your breathing as your focus, you'd do the same thing. Is it fast or slow? Are you taking deep or shallow breaths? Is it labored or easy? Does the air feel cool or warm as it enters your lungs? And so on.

A variation of this is observing your thoughts. Basically, you visualize yourself sitting at the bottom of a body of water, like a lake. From this visualized position, you then imagine your thoughts bubbling up one at a time in front of you.

The amount of time this bubble remains in your awareness is approximately 6-8 seconds, basically how long it takes to form, start rising, and eventually moving outside your range of awareness. There's no analysis of this thought bubble, just a detached observation as it passes through your field of awareness.

It's fine if the same thought goes past numerous times as long as you don't become attached to it or explore it for some deeper meaning. The whole point of the exercise is to just be able to observe the thought bubbling by without attachment.

Guided/Unguided

The next category of meditation is guided or unguided. This category is pretty straight forward. Neither one is better or worse, but depending on your goals, one may work better than the other for a specific task.

With a guided meditation, you usually have a very specific, easily definable goal to work with. With that goal firmly in mind, you develop a script to guide your internal visualization down the path you choose. In the beginning, I suggest using prerecorded guided meditations or sitting in on a live guided meditation.

Only after experiencing a number of guided meditations would I suggest crafting your own, if for no other reason than to keep from following an ineffective meditation that may steer you down the wrong path.

With guided meditation, because you're strongly tapping into your creative, visual side of your mind, the imagery you choose can have a strong effect on your inner environment. Every mental image you visualize can and will stir up specific mental reactions that may or may not be beneficial.

That's why you want to start with either a guide or a prerecorded session. Then you can safely experience what a good guided meditation feels like. That way, when you start scripting your own, you'll be able to tell intuitively whether it's going to help you accomplish your goals.

On the flip side of things, an unstructured meditation can be of benefit when you're casting about for ideas but you don't have any preconceived notions of what they should be.

A good example of this goes back to the previous category and the bubble meditation. You practice it by just being and observing your thoughts as that pass on by. You don't try to have a specific train of thought go by. You just let come what may.

In the chapter on sample meditations, I'll cover a kind of hybrid version of this meditation category called image streaming. It's basically starting with a specific thought and instructing your subconscious mind to lead you to an answer you're trying to find. It can be very helpful if you've accidentally written yourself into a dead end and aren't sure how to write your way back out, among other things.

Verbal/Nonverbal

The next category is whether there verbal components to your meditation or not. This category is what most people are familiar with when they think of meditation.

The image that springs to mind of most people is the quintessential bald-headed monk in robes sitting on a mat repeatedly going "OOOMMMMM" for hours at a stretch. Believe it or not, there's quite a few other meditations that actually uses words or phrases while meditating.

What I think about when it comes to verbal/vocal meditations comes from Wayne Dyer's program The Secrets to Manifesting Your Destiny. In that audio program, he teaches several vocal sounds to intone during your meditation. You can also find it in book form but I don't feel you'll get as much out of it since you don't hear the tones he demonstrates in the audio program.

The vibrations that are generated in your body from doing the tones correctly can actually have a strong impact on your health, focus, mental clarity, and general well-being. It's something you'd have to experience to understand it. I've practiced it on and off for a while and I did notice a difference my life, but I'm not that partial to making noises while meditating. I prefer peace and quiet when trying to get in touch with my inner self.

Obviously, a nonverbal type of meditation is what I was just describing. You don't purposely make any type of vocal utterance of any sort while meditating, other than certain types of breathing patterns, like when you're doing certain yoga postures.

You just allow the quiet of your surroundings help you focus on your particular meditative path for the day. The stillness can help deepen your concentration and greatly enrich your experience in the now.

I do know that some people out there that go stir crazy without some type of noise or sound. Short of having a recording going in the background, maybe some classical baroque music or a guided meditation with soft background music, some type of verbal/vocal type of meditation may be the best style to work with for these types of personalities.

Moving/Stationary

The final category falls under moving and stationary forms of meditation. This is the category that I bounce back and forth between depending on my mood.

A moving meditation focuses on observing how your body feels as it goes through some form of movement. It can be a very structured movement, like Tai-Chi or yoga, or it could be a very unstructured form, like some type of expressionistic dance.

Another possible purpose for the movement may deal with directing your internal energy (Chi, Qi, Ki, Prana,Kundalini, subtle body, etc) a certain way throughout the body. Tai-Chi and some forms of Chi-Gung (qigong) specifically focus on this aspect of moving meditation.

In my story in Appendix A, it was a very specific type of Chi-Gung that I practiced that allowed me to function on such a reduced amount of rest because of how much internal energy it generated, along with the level of relaxation and well-being I felt after each session.

Stationary forms of meditation obviously means you're not moving. The vision of the monk meditating on a rug is an example of this type of meditation. In the book The Way of Energy, it describes what, for the most part, is a stationary form of Chi-Gung meditation. There are five body positions that you train in that, over time, you learn to link in a very specific order to circulate your Chi efficiently throughout the body. You maintain each posture for at least 5-10 minutes.

When I was much younger, I would spend 30-45 minutes doing this form of standing meditation. I was also studying Shaolin Kempo Karate at the same time. The strong foundation I built practicing that form of standing meditation made it very difficult to off-balance me, either mentally or physically, during sparring practice. It was, and is, a very enjoyable type of meditation.

Time commitment

The biggest downside, if you want to consider it that way, is the time commitment needed to start experiencing the benefits listed earlier. This isn't a quick fix type process, but a lifelong journey that deepens the longer you practice it.

You get out of it what you put into it. But there are other options available to you if you need something now, if not sooner. They do have pros and cons that you don't need to really worry about when following a traditional meditative path, but if used carefully, may make a noticeable difference very quickly.

If you practice a traditional style of meditation in conjunction with the following technological tools, you can basically negate a lot of the possible negatives that you might experience using technological tools alone. Meditation and technology can work in a very synergistic manner under these circumstances.

CHAPTER 5

TECHNOLOGY

Ah... technology... What can't it do? There are quite a few technologies out there currently that let you obtain, within 5-10 minutes, the same level of focus and lower brain-wave states that a yogi or monk would, with decades of experience, take 20-30 minutes to reach. Even better, you'll be able to maintain these levels longer and more easily than a yogi or monk would be able to accomplish.

With just the push of a button, you'll be able to effortlessly drop into the coveted Alpha/Theta state and stay there for extended periods of time. After a little bit of time, you might even be able to say bye bye to caffeinated drinks because you'll no longer need them to become alert, energized, and raring to go.

PROS/CONS OF USING TECHNOLOGY

What's not to like? Actually, with few exceptions, there's very little downside to such an accelerated path to "mastery". The biggest pitfalls actually fall into 3 categories:

- The tendency, at least in the beginning, to fall asleep

- Possible headaches

- Dredging up of emotional "land-mines" that you're not fully
  equipped to handle

That last one is quite significant, actually. With some of these technologies, you're going to be directly simulating and modifying your conscious brain patterns. This modification may, in certain individuals, generate mental, emotional, and physical experiences that you're not equipped to handle.

Bill Harris, the founder of Centerpointe Research Institute and creator of one of the technologies I'll be covering called Holosync®, gave his personal experience of what happens when you advance too quickly through the process before you're ready. If you're interested, it's in his book Thresholds of the Mind, on page 39. Suffice it to say, he almost became an emotional wreck.

For this reason, if you have any concerns or questions, I highly recommend talking to a doctor or psychologist first before using this type of technological help. With that being said, a majority of you who try experimenting with these tools will only experience the positive effects and benefits that I've listed previously.

TYPES OF TECHNOLOGY

First off, if you want to research this topic more on your own, you need to know what the process is called. The technical term for what all these technologies do is called entrainment, more specifically brain-wave entrainment.

Per Wikipedia©, "Brain-wave Entrainment is any practice that aims to cause brain-wave frequencies to fall into step with a periodic stimulus having a frequency corresponding to the intended brain-state.[1]" It goes on to state, "… the human brain has a tendency to change its dominant EEG frequency towards the frequency of a dominant external stimulus." In other words,

1   Wikipedia, http://en.wikipedia.org/wiki/Brainwave_entrainment

subject it to a certain frequency the right way, your brain will start to match that frequency.

Generally speaking, these tools fall under one of three categories, but they can, and usually do, cover more than one category.

The three categories are:

- Aural - sound based

- Visual - vision based

- Kinesthetic - touch based

While I'm going to cover all three categories, I'm going to spend the most time on the aural category because it has the most options available to implement it. The other reason is because the visual one blocks your vision, making it difficult to write, and the kinesthetic option, if you can find the equipment, requires focus to get the most benefit from, focus that would draw you away from the writing process.

They would be good options to test before you start writing though.

Aural

The most utilized modality for entrainment is the aural category. In fact, there's more types of technology based off of sound than the other two categories combined.

There's a good reason for it, too. You have a much wider range of frequencies, tones, and patterns to work with as opposed to visual or kinesthetic modalities.

Binaural beats

The most widely used method of audible entrainment is called binaural beats. This technology is based off of the process of providing a specific tones in each ear, called the carrier tones, which in turn causes the brain to generate a third, internal tone called the beat frequency.

What happens in the brain is, when you hear two separate tones, one for each ear, as long as the frequency difference between the two isn't that big, your brain will start to resonate with a phantom third frequency. This phantom frequency is equivalent to the difference between the two carrier frequencies.

For example, if your left ear is hearing a 550Hz tone, and your right ear is hearing a 560Hz tone, your brain will start to resonate at 10Hz, or the difference between the left and right ears.

If you remember what I covered earlier in the chapter on brain-wave levels, you'll notice this is smack dab in the middle of the Alpha brain-wave frequency. To take this further, by listening to the two different tones, you are in fact forcing your brain to fall into an Alpha brain-wave pattern.

Now most programs will also induce, to a greater or lesser degree, some of the other 3 brain-wave frequencies as well. How much of each is dependent on the company providing the soundtrack.

The main downside is, you need to listen to them with stereo headphones to be effective. Also, they need to be good quality headphones. The higher the quality, the better binaural beat recordings work. It comes down the accuracy and frequency response of the headset.

If the quality of the headset is poor in general or they have a poor frequency response, you're not going to get as pure of a tone reproduction. While this doesn't usually matter with regular music, it makes a world of difference with binaural beats.

To give you an idea of what I mean, I have a set of Sennheiser® headphones that cost around $200. Before that, I had some ear buds that cost around $50. I can notice a huge difference between the two headsets when it comes to the effects of my binaural beat recordings. It matters that much.

HemiSync

The company that really started the ball rolling for this type of self-improvement was The Monroe Institute®, formed by Robert Monroe. As far back as 1956, Robert had been experimenting with the binaural beat effect, creating what would eventually be called Hemi-Sync®.

Quite honestly, I don't have much experience with their products, so I honestly can't say how effective they are. I do know that they offer a wide range of binaural beat audio programs, guided meditation programs, and visual meditations programs.

As one of the companies that have been in the field the longest, they have quite a bit to offer someone who wants to explore this area of self-improvement.

Holosync

Next up is the Centerpointe Research Institute with their HoloSync® technology. Created in 1989, they were the first company to make the connection between carrier frequencies and how effective a binaural beat program was. They determined that the lower the carrier frequencies were, the stronger the effect the audio program had.

I've had more experience with their technology, but in an indirect manner. What I mean by this is the next technology I'm going to discuss actually licenses the HoloSync® technology for their own use.

Paraliminal

Learning Strategies is the company that I've had the most experience with, by far. Over the years, I've probably spent well over $1,000 acquiring their various programs.

The programs that I'm going to talk about specifically here are called Paraliminal® recordings. Paraliminals® are not to be confused with subliminal recordings. With subliminal recordings, you're not consciously aware of the message being delivered to your subconscious.

Paraliminals®, on the other hand, work off of a different mechanism, namely using Neuro-linguistic programming (NLP) to provide the primary benefit. Basically, what happens is that they play a verbal track in one ear using language geared for the logical side of the mind. In the other ear, they use language geared towards the creative side of the mind.

It's fundamentally the same message, but utilizing the left brain/right brain structure, providing a verbal message that each side of the mind will understand better.

I first got involved with their technology back in 2001-2002. The reason this is important is back then, that's the extent of the Paraliminal® technology. Two verbal audio tracks played at the same time.

Now there's no way to prove it, but after playing around with both a sample HoloSync® program disc and a couple full-fledged Paraliminal® recordings, I went on their website and asked what, to me anyway, was a pretty basic question. If Paraliminals® work best when you're at Alpha level and HoloSync® mechanically forces you to that level, why don't you combine the two.

A few years later, I heard that Learning Strategies had released an update to an unrelated program I had, so I got back in touch and got the new update. With the updated program they also provided an updated version of the Paraliminal® recording that came with the original program. The difference being, it now had the HoloSync® audio technology playing as the background tone.

So did they take my suggestion, or did they realize it on their own at about the same time, I'll never know. What I do know is that with the merging of the two technologies, you get a very powerful audio recording that can specifically target the areas you want to improve.

For the purpose of increasing your creativity, reducing stress, and getting past writer's block, I suggest the following programs:

- Anxiety-Free: Help overcome anxiety and stress which is one of the main sources of writer's block

- Personal Genius: Geared specifically to unlock your ability to come up with creative solutions to problems

- Peak Performance: Self explanatory

- Get Around to it: Overcoming procrastination

For more specific things indirectly dealing with writing:

- 10-Minute Supercharger: Just as good as a cup of coffee without the jitters

- Dream Play: Helping you unlock the power of your sleeping
  dream state to overcome problems, be more creative, and remember what you dreamed

- Deep Relaxation: Self explanatory

With these 7 program recordings, you should be able to overcome just about any issue that might arise with your writing time. I love my Paraliminals® and wouldn't ever want to lose access to them.

Isochronic beats

The next type of audio entrainment technology is called isochronic tones. Whereas with binaural beats you use two tones to create a resonant phantom tone, isochronic beats use one clear tone, pulsed at the resonant frequency, to induce the desired brain-wave state.

In other words, if you want to cause your brain to go into the Alpha brain-wave state at 10Hz, you would have one tone that pulses at 10Hz. It's pretty straight forward. It really is as simple and straight forward as that.

What this means is, you don't need an expensive headset, or any type of headset for that matter, to experience the benefits. You could listen to them on a decent stereo. It also means you can share it with friends that come over by playing it on the stereo so everyone can hear it. You just can't do that with a binaural beat based program.

There's also anecdotal evidence that suggests that it's actually a more effective technology than binaural beats as well. It's less distracting, more effective, and the audio equipment requirements to utilize are less expensive.

The main downsides are, compared to the actual cost for a binaural recording, an isochronic recording is going to be slightly more expensive. The other downside is that, as far as I could find doing a quick search on the Internet, there seems to really be only one company that provides any programs based on this technology.

What this means is that you have a much smaller selection of available recordings compared to what's available in the binaural beat market. This might not necessarily be a bad thing, but it's something to keep in mind.

The Unexplainable Store

The only website that I found that had any amount of isochronic type recordings was a site called the Unexplainable Store (http://www.unexplainablestore.com/). They seem to have a decent selection of recording that are geared to specific results, so they might have a large enough selection to cover what you need.

Visual

The next area of entrainment technology is visual entrainment. These tools are usually bundled with equipment that also plays some form of binaural beat program at the same time.

This technology works by flashing pulses of lights in front of your closed eyes at a pace/frequency that's equivalent of the brain-wave state you're trying to reach.

The equipment that flashes the light is usually some type of goggle or eyeglass type setup. The cheaper ones I've seen look like regular sunglasses that have lights drilled and glued into the lenses.

The more expensive ones are more like welder's goggles, meaning they block out all light except the flashes produced by the machine, increasing its effectiveness.

When sold as a kit with an audio machine, they're usually marketed as a meditation machine. The goggles pulse at the same frequency as the phantom beat, amplifying and building off of each other synergistically.

This technology can be pretty effective since your visual senses are pretty responsive to outside stimulus. The main downside, and it really can be significant, is that some people can go into seizures due to the flashing light frequencies produced.

It's because of this possible effect that I usually steer people away from them unless they know for sure that they don't have this issue, but not everyone realizes they are susceptible to seizures until it happens.

Unless you have a really strong reason to use it, I would suggest staying away from this technology until you've determined you're not getting much benefit from the other programs that are available.

Kinesthetic

The final area of entrainment deals with kinesthetic feedback. Now a true kinesthetic device is difficult to find and might not really be that effective. What you're really looking for is a device called a biofeedback machine.

What this equipment does is measure the galvanic response of your skin, I.E. how well it conducts/resists electricity, and provides some type of audible or visual feedback on the results.

With the feedback provided, a user can eventually control their body's level of stress, meaning they can lower their level of stress consciously with just a little effort.

Once you can consciously control your level of stress, you can more easily relax, which in turn lets you get closer to the brainwave states that increase creativity.

USE BEFORE OR DURING WRITING

Some of these technologies work well and are best used just before writing since they induce relaxation, help expand your creativity, and basically allow you to focus more easily on the writing job at hand.

Other programs can be used while actually writing, allowing you to maintain a high level of focus for an extended length of time with very little effort. For parts of this book, I used a software program on my phone to generate a Theta frequency that I listened to while writing.

To give you an idea of how well it worked, I was able to write close to 1,000 words in about 45 minutes while doing research on where to find some of these technologies. I didn't even realize how long I was working until I looked down at the clock. If I hadn't looked, I probably would have been able to write non-stop for at least 2-3 hours like I have in the past.

Another indirect benefit of using an audio based program is that it helps drown out external noises and distractions. So when you can't get away from it all, you can shield yourself from it to a point where it's the next best thing.

CHAPTER 6

A FEW SAMPLE STYLES OF MEDITATION

While I've tried to give a good overview of what kind of benefits you can expect from meditation and how it can help you overcome writer's block while also increasing your creativity, the one thing I really can't do is give an exhaustive review of all the different types and forms of meditation that's available out there.

What I can do is give a quick overview of a couple of styles that I currently practice, how to get more in-depth information on how practicing it, and/or get the optional equipment to perform it correctly.

First off, the type of meditation I do most frequently and have practiced the longest is the one taught by José Silva, called the Silva Mind Control Method. Before you get the wrong idea, José meant mind control from the perspective of teaching you how to control *your* mind, not someone else's.

The beauty of this system is that it's very easy to follow, provides fast results, and its initial goal for you is to actually reach the Alpha level. Some of the affirmations you tell yourself actually reinforce your intention to reach Alpha level. Based off the progression speed of the program, you should be starting to consistently reach Alpha level within 30 days, often in less than a minute under the right conditions.

At the heart of most mind exploration programs that don't have an 'ancient' lineage — along with a lot of self-hypnosis programs — work by doing a reverse countdown until you hit one or zero. After doing this for a number of repetitions, your body develops a 'muscle-memory' or habit that says, when I count down in this particular manner, I'm trying to accomplish X. Other programs visualize having you walk down flights of stairs, or riding an elevator down, in the effort to convey to your subconscious mind what you're trying to accomplish, mainly relax enough to reach the Alpha level.

One other important bit to keep in mind is that your mind, at the Alpha level, won't let you have or recognize negative based language. In other words, one of the things that people practice the Silva method for is to lose weight. If you try to use the affirmation, "I don't want to be fat", your subconscious mind will ignore all the language with negative connotations. In fact, it might snap you out of the Alpha level entirely.

If it doesn't snap you out of Alpha level, with an affirmation of, "I don't want to be fat," the way your subconscious would decode it is, "I want to be fat." Granted, this is an oversimplification of the process, the depth of which would be a book unto itself. In fact, there are several.

As a personal example, at one point in my life, I weighed 255lb. I realized that I was in pain a lot of the time and didn't really feel good about myself. So for one week, I used the Silva method to talk to my subconscious mind and let it know that I didn't want to be that size/weight any more. Instead, I told/ visualized to my subconscious that I wanted to be around 220lb.

After only doing that for a week, I stopped and didn't think about it anymore. With no conscious effort on my part, I dropped down to that weight within approximately 6 months. I didn't exercise more, nor did I try and control my portion size. It just slowly dropped off on its own. I've now been at that weight, give or take 5lb, for over the past 10 years.

The downside to this is that now, even though I'd much rather be around 205lb, I've been stuck at 225lb. No matter what I physically try — weight lifting, aerobics, portion control, etc. — I haven't been able to budge my weight more than a couple pounds, and only for a short period of time. I just haven't built up enough desire to focus on another week long Silva session to try and change my subconscious programming. I have too many other, more important, things to focus on.

The other bit to keep in mind is that your subconscious prefers to communicate in pictures. It has a very limited ability to communicate in words, so verbal affirmations will have some effect, but being able to strongly visualize your goals will go a long way towards actually helping you reach them.

With that, let's begin discussing different forms of meditation.

The Silva Method - A brief overview

The basis of the program starts your initial practice when you first wake up in the morning. Once you are skilled with the process, you can perform it at any time. To begin, the steps are:

1. Wake up

2. Go to the bathroom if needed and then crawl back into bed

3. Set your alarm in case you fall back to sleep. A good starting time is 15 minutes

4. Close your eyes and look 'up' approximately 20 degrees higher than straight ahead (there's a reason for this that I'll cover in the odds and ends chapter)

5. For the first ten days, count down from 100 to 1 at approximately a 2 second interval.

6. Assuming you don't fall asleep and you focus on the counting and desired results, by the time you reach 1, you should be at Alpha level.

That's it. There's also a specific process to bring yourself out of the Alpha state, but even if you did nothing, the alarm clock or the passage of time would eventually bring you out of it as well. To bring yourself out manually, you would count from 1 to 5, giving mental affirmations that you're becoming more conscious and aware and feeling great. At the number 5, you should be fully awake and aware.

Over the proceeding days, at each 10 day mark, you slowly reduce the number you start at, like for the second 10 days, you start at 50, and so on. Eventually, you'll reach the point where you're going from 5 to 1. At that point, you've developed enough mastery to be able to reach the Alpha level when desired by just following the 5 to one process.

The reason you initially start practicing first thing in the morning is because you are just coming out of your natural Alpha state, which you naturally pass through when going from sleeping to waking.

Without going into the underlying mechanics of the process, it's always easier to teach you new skill when you can link it to an already known skill, so linking the countdown to a period where you're already at an Alpha level just allows you to link the two together quickly and easily.

4-count meditation

Another form of meditation you can practice is similar to the one you're pretty familiar with if you've followed along up to this point.

It's pretty straight forward and is probably the most basic of meditations you can practice, but by no means is it less effective than any other forms of meditation.

To do it, you:

1. Find a spot to comfortably sit or lie down. If you have back issues like me, you might want to sit on a pillow or have some sort of back support to lean against.

2. Close your eyes (you can do it with your eyes open, but it cuts down on distractions if you close them until you've developed some experience)

3. Breath in deep through your nose, focusing on bringing the breath as deep into the lower part of your lungs as possible, filling them to about 90% capacity. You don't want to strain to reach this point, so at any time you start to have difficulty breathing in this deeply, back off. Work up to this level.

4. Hold your breath for a few seconds.

5. Breathe out through your slightly pursed lips until you've exhaled as much as you comfortably can. Some versions also recommend touching the tip of your tongue to the roof

of your mouth slightly behind your teeth. The reason for this stems from the theory of closing the circuit through which your vital essence flows through. Not a requirement, but something to think about.

6.   Pause for a couple seconds.

7.   Repeat.

While doing this cycle/process, you're going to count from 1 to 4 with each cycle. Once you hit 4, on the next cycle, you'll start at 1 again. It doesn't matter if you're counting on the inhale or exhale as long as you're counting at the same spot.

For the first time, you'll want to limit your practice to around 5 minutes. If you can't go that long, it's fine. Go as long as you can. If you feel comfortable at this point, it's also OK to go longer.

You're goal it to work up to 15 minutes to a half hour for each session, but don't force it. This meditation practice is pretty much the basis for most other forms of seated/stationary type of meditative practices.

Walking/Running meditation

When I was in better shape, I used to practice this type of meditation a lot. If you want to look into it further, I suggest checking out Chirunning and Chiwalking.

To try a basic variation of it is pretty simple. If you looked at the previous meditation, all you're really going to do is perform a variation of the process.

While walking, jogging, or running, you're going to focus on how you feel, how your body is performing, all the little nuances that you normally try to block out while walking or running. You're going to focus your attention internally to really 'feel' what your body is doing.

You're basically just observing how your body is operating while running, how it feels each time your foot touches the pavement, how it feels to have the air flow into the body, how it feels to exhale, and how it feels to just move through space.

This introspection is what is going to allow you to go inside and build up that body/mind connection, helping you reduce stress and improve your connection to your inner mind.

Like other forms of meditation, in the beginning, you'll be easily distracted by a multitude of things, but over time, you'll learn to focus on just this moment in time and how it feels to just 'be'. Another term for this state is mindfulness.

This type of mediation helps clear out all the stress and anxiety you might have about your writing through introspection and physical movement/exercise, allowing you to come back to it with a clear head and reduced stress. It also helps increase the amount of oxygen in your bloodstream.

Other forms to pursue

Like I said, there's a bunch of other methods you can practice and I encourage you to dig into the subject further. Beyond getting past writer's block and developing more creativity, adding some form of meditation to your lifestyle can add years to your life, more enjoyment to the years you have, and allow you to more fully enjoy the simpler things in life. What more could you ask for?

If you're interested, and for further study, check out some of the books in the bibliography. I'm sure you'll find something of interest to pursue further.

CHAPTER 7

ODDS AND ENDS

This chapter was kind of added after I had created a basic outline for this book. I debated on whether to add it or not. Most of what's in this chapter has nothing to do with meditation directly, but they are things I've learned over the years to help with overcoming writer's block, accelerated learning, and improved memory retention. Basically, how to learn stuff faster and remember it longer.

Most of the stuff you're taught in school on how to learn something is just plain wrong or inefficient. A lot of what you were taught actually interferes with the learning process and makes it harder to learn new things. I'm not saying it's all totally worthless (I still use traditional note taking methods from time to time), but there are much more efficient and effective ways to learn and organize information.

There's also tricks here to help improve the effectiveness of your meditative practice that doesn't belong to any specific style of practice. They're stand-alone tips that draw from neuroscience and NLP.

Eye position

Although all I could really find is mostly anecdotal evidence to back this up, I was able to locate one thesis paper on the subject. The thesis paper was entitled, "What life can compare with this? Sitting alone at the window, I watch the flowers bloom, the leaves fall, the seasons come and go." By Howard Rheingold. It was near the bottom on page 32.[1] During their study, they discovered that with the subject lifting their gaze, it induced Alpha brain-waves. In addition to this thesis, there are several programs I use that point to this phenomena as well.

In The Silva Mind Control Method book, on page 30, José mentions that for reasons not entirely known, raising your eyes by 20-45 degrees seems to stimulate the production of Alpha waves. Through all of the Paraliminal® programs, they don't tell you why, but they do instruct you to look up higher than straight ahead viewing.

Something else that may be related to this effect comes from Neuro-Linguist Programming (NLP). In NLP, they've determined that when you're trying to access your visual centers of your brain, you normally look up.

For a majority of right handed people (it can sometimes flip-flop, but there would be other indicators that would indicate this is the case), when you look up and to your left, you access the parts of the mind that deal with visual remembered information, like what your living room looks like.

When you look up and to your right, on the other hand, it's accessing the visual created section of your mind, I.E. your imagination. An example would be trying to imagine what it would look like to have a large polka-dotted elephant in your living room watching TV. So if you're trying to come up with something creative, looking up to your right might be the best bet. If you're doing it during meditation, then you're also going to generate more Alpha brain-waves.

---

1   www.rheingold.com/texts/HowardRheingoldReedthesis.pdf

Mind Mapping

While this isn't a meditative practice, it's a method to help overcome writer's block and help with creativity. Mind mapping is a way to help your mind pull information out of your unconscious memory and provide a very loose framework upon which to deposit the information you pull into the conscious mind.

I'm only going to provide a very brief idea of how to do a mind map. Because of the breadth of information this topic covers, it makes it impractical to try and do more than just provide an overview of the process.

Basically, you put a word or two in the center of the page. These words should relate to what you're trying to organize information about. Usually you want it to be the main topic, but it's possible to break off one of the sub topics from a larger map and proceed to mind map from there.

Once you have this main circle in the center, you start to plot down ideas/draw circles around the main idea, adding words and snippets that relate to the central circle. As you develop your map, you'll start to see linkages between different ideas that might be worth exploring.

For example, a mind map for this book would have been:

— How to break through Writer's block (center)

Then ideas that could go around it:

- Relaxation
- Brainstorming
- Meditation

- Brain-wave states

- Reading works similar to what I want to write

- Audio programs

- What's already been covered

From there, I could see that there's a link between relaxation and meditation. I also know that during meditation, there's a change in my brain-wave state. I know that certain audio programs can induce relaxation and altered brain-wave activity. I know that I haven't come across any other books on writing that addresses writer's block from that perspective. And so on.

It's kinda like brainstorming except that you're guiding the creative process by having a central idea and coming up with stuff that circles around that central idea. You also have the ability to branch off from any of the other circles with other thoughts that are all related/can be grouped under that sub-circle.

It's an easy way to organize data and provide a more structured form for your research notes. It may help spark some of your creativity by helping you see linkages between things that, at first glance, are completely unrelated.

Image streaming

Image streaming is almost, but not entirely, like meditation. More specifically, it strongly resembles a guided meditation session. The main difference is, you're going to use a tape recorder to record you describing what you're "seeing" in your mind's eye instead of listening to a recording or script that guides you through the process.

The exercise comes from the book, <u>The Einstein Factor</u>, by Win Wenger. Basically, you sit in a comfortable position, close your eyes, and start describing what come up in your mind's eye. The trick is, you have to describe them out loud, hence the audio recorder.

You have to use all 5 senses to describe what you're seeing/ experiencing. Finally, you have to phrase EVERYTHING in the present tense.

In and of itself, it can help you greatly improve your creativity levels. Preliminary studies have shown that people who do image streaming can actually raise their I.Q. by several points, averaging approximately .9 I.Q. points per hour of practice, or a full point every 80 minutes.

Another benefit of image streaming, because you're developing stronger connections to your subconscious mind by working with images, is that you can use it to solve problems.

One method is to visualize coming across some type of container, like an egg. While examining this container, KNOW that the answer to your problem is contained inside the container. When you really know it's in the container, you open it to see what the solution is.

It gives your subconscious mind the instruction to find an answer to your problem and it provides your subconscious mind a place to put said solution in a place your conscious mind is looking. Granted, the answer is going to be in the form of a visualization, but if you review your recording when you're done, you'll find you have a good idea of what the solution is, or how to pursue it further.

"Putting on Heads"

Another helpful exercise from <u>The Einstein Factor</u>, and covered in much greater depth in Burt Goldman's "Quantum Jumping" programs, is a technique called "Swapping Heads".

The basic process is to get yourself in an Alpha brain-wave state through meditation or audio recording. You then, depending on the program, visualize yourself coming across an "alternate dimension" version of yourself that's highly skilled in an area you want to develop more fully. After meeting your alternative self and discussing what you're there to learn, you enter into your doppelgänger's body, either by turning into a ghost and floating into it or by actually putting the body on like a costume, and see/feel what it's like to be that alternative self.

Once you've experienced how to perform like your doppelgänger, you exit your alternative self, thank them, and then bring yourself back to conscious level. Once you're at conscious level, you should practice the skill as soon as possible, if not immediately, to lock in the skill you just "learned."

Surprisingly enough, there's a lot of studies that show that, through some mechanism, the mind is able to teach these types of skills. There's examples of people who don't think they have artistic talent being placed under deep hypnosis and told they're famous artists. Then they're told to create a new masterpiece. After they've finished, what they created usually is a highly skilled, highly professional piece of work. When the people who were under deep hypnosis are told they created it, they will flatly refuse to believe it unless it's proven to them.

What's more interesting is that after these sessions, the subjects tend to have higher levels of that skill than they did before the sessions. "Putting on Heads" provides you a means to take advantage of this effect without going to a hypnotherapist.

The habit of writing every day

This topic has been beaten to death in most books on writing. They all state how important it is to get into the habit of writing every, but never really touch on why, or if they do, they just kinda gloss over it. Developing the habit of writing every day, or at least on the same day at the same time, really can make a difference in your ability to get past writer's block, as all the other writing experts can attest to.

Developing a habit of writing works so well because of a few different reasons though. The biggest one is that, through repetition, you get used to doing the thing you're trying to develop the habit for, in this case writing. What's less noticed is what a habit actually does for the person who's developing the habit.

A habit, when properly formed, allows the conscious mind to relax more because it doesn't have to think through every step of the process you're developing the habit for. In computer terms, the time you spend creating the habit would be similar to actually writing the program: creating the original program, debugging it, looking for sections that might make the program function less effectively, etc. Once you've polished the program to the point where it's working like you want, you save it for when you need it.

The next time you come across a situation where that habit would help, you "load up" the program and run it, allowing it to do its thing, until it's not needed anymore. Then the program ends and waits until it's needed again.

The other thing about a habit is that, because it becomes second nature, you're less stressed about the situation you developed the habit for. You're more sure of yourself and not stressing about the unknowns in a situation. As we've already covered, the less stressed you are, the more easily you can access your creative abilities.

So by creating a habit of writing consistently, you allow your conscious mind to relax because it's familiar with the situation, thereby allowing you to more readily access your creative muse. The more often you reinforce this habit, the more relaxed you'll get for each session. So do what all the other writing experts advise and make writing a daily habit. It'll make it harder and harder for writer's block to rear its ugly head.

5-point essay

Another tool that most writers, especially nonfiction and informational writers, shouldn't be without is a means to create an outline of their writing project.

For me, the five paragraph expository writing format is perfect. With it, you can create a fast outline 'skeleton' to hang your information from. Let me put to rest that it won't hamper creativity in the slightest if you use it correctly. It's just a loose framework tool to help you organize your thoughts and to add clarity to your writing.

It follows the adage of:

- Tell them what your going to tell them

- Tell them

- Tell them what you told them

Just with the basic outline, you can usually create article length copy in relatively short order. So if you're doing things like creating articles for publication, informative blog posts, and similar writing projects, just following this format will have you cranking out the material relatively quickly.

In a nutshell, the format is:

- First paragraph - introduction to the topic you're going to cover

- Second paragraph - first point to cover

- Third paragraph - second point to cover

- Fourth paragraph - third point to cover

- Fifth paragraph - conclusion

You can usually expand any of the paragraphs to an extent to provide more related information on that topic, but you only want to have one idea per paragraph section.

Where the power of this comes into play is when you have to write longer pieces. With the basic outline, the format is:

- Opening

- 3 points
- Closing

With the outline to expand it to the size you need, it becomes:

1. Opening
2. Point 1
   - 2.1.   Sub-point 1
   - 2.2.   Sub-point 2
   - 2.3.   Sub-point 3
3. Point 2
   - 3.1.   Sub-point 1
   - 3.2.   Sub-point 2
   - 3.3.   Sub-point 3
4. Point 3
   - 4.1.   Sub-point 1
   - 4.2.   Sub-point 2
   - 4.3.   Sub-point 3
5. Closing

That layout can get you somewhere in the 8,000-10,000 word count range. Going one level deeper could get you significantly higher. This book itself was outlined very loosely using this format and I was able to get over 15,000 words out of it very easily. Because I had an outline to work from, I knew where I was going at any point along the journey. Having an idea of where your headed allows you to bypass writer's block relatively easily.

It's just a tool to allow you to focus more on your writing opposed to something that locks you in to a preordained layout. When your original layout doesn't help you progress along, redo it or throw it out. Don't let a preconceived notion about what it's for slow your writing down.

Diet/Nutrition

As a final point, I'd be remiss if I didn't touch on diet, exercise, nutrition, and how it can affect your writing, energy level, and creativity. I'm not going to beat you over the head and say one diet is better than another or that if you don't do "X" a certain amount, you're a failure. I'm just going to point out some basic common sense stuff that you might never have thought of in this perspective before.

First and foremost, exercise. Now I'm not talking about hitting the gym a bunch during the week and taking on a resemblance to the incredible hulk. What I am going to say is that when you exercise, you absorb more oxygen into your blood stream. Exercise in this respect could be a brisk 5-10 minute walk around the block, some fast jump-roping in the driveway, some calisthenics, or even jumping jack would suffice. We're just looking for something to get your body revved up a little to improve blood flow and oxygen levels. The more blood and oxygen to the brain, the better and more clearly you'll be able to think and concentrate on the job at hand.

For diet, same simple things. Try not to drink sugary drinks or greasy foods. Those spikes of sugar and grease are going to throw off your body because of sugar spiking/crashing and general feelings of sluggishness as your body tries to process this stuff. If you need stuff to drink before and during writing, water is always the best answer. If you need caffeine, try drinking coffee without a lot of sugar or creamer. The amount of sugar/creamer can offset the benefits of the caffeine in the coffee when it comes to alertness/concentration levels.

Tea is marginally better and preferred by people who don't like the harsh flavor of unsweetened coffee. Adding a dollop of honey is fine with tea since honey is processed more slowly by the body, meaning a more gradual sugar spike. It doesn't mean load it down with honey since it will still cause a sugar spike, just that it's more manageable.

On the topic of sweeteners. Unless you have a good medical reason for it, ***stay away from artificial sweeteners like the plague***. None of them are good for you regardless of what the advertising says. Unless it's 100% natural, your body is going to have a hard time processing it. Since these artificial sweeteners don't occurred in nature, your body doesn't know what to do with it once it enters the body. This confusion may make the body more sluggish, cause weight gain, mental confusion, and other detrimental side effects.

The more natural you can make your diet, the better overall your body will function. The better it functions, the less strain there is on it and the better your brain works. With a better diet, your body has more nutrients getting to it, is producing less toxins from having to deal with artificial ingredients, and overall, you'll just feel better and have more energy.

Notice that nowhere in there did I say what you can and can't have food-wise, other than trying to stay away from artificial sweeteners and other fake ingredients. You'll feel better in the long term.

One final thing I would like to touch on deals with energy drinks. Due to my hyperactivity, I don't drink them because they have absolutely no effect on me. With that being said, I know a lot of people swear by them. The problem is, they're mostly sugar, artificial sweeteners, and caffeine in a concentrated form. I've already gone over why those things are bad in general, but energy drinks are worse. Because they're in such a concentrated form, people have a tendency to ingest way more than what, with tongue firmly in cheek, is healthy for them. People treat them like soda, but because of the caffeine content, it can be dangerous to drink more than one or two a day. There's research coming out, if you care to do a search on Google®, that shows it adversely impacting cardiovascular health in general and in extreme cases, causing heart attacks. Just something to think about before you crack open that case of Monster® before settling down to write.

CHAPTER 8

In Closing

Hopefully something here will strike a chord with you and entice you to look into some form of meditation as a way of life and as a tool to help break through writer's block. A lot of professional writers will tell you that it's a lack of focus, or unclear thinking, or something very similar. To a degree, I agree with them. Where I don't agree is that writer's block is in some way only related to having a lack of motivation or just being lazy.

I've seen quite a few books on writing that all but come right out and say that there's no such thing as writer's block and that it's just a cop-out. I don't believe that either.

Sure, all this can have an effect on your writing ability, but I think your anxiety and stress levels play a very important role in creating writer's block due to the shift in brain-wave patterns this stress causes.

I think a lot of the writers that state there's no such thing as writer's block, that it's all about sitting down, buckling down, and writing, whether consciously or unconsciously, have learned how to mentally relax, allowing the creative centers of their mind to open and allow ideas to flow freely from head to paper.

What I hope you get out of this book is that there's exercises and tools that can help you get to the same level of relaxation, removing the disruptive tensions, and allowing you to tap into the creative muse that exists inside all of us.

I ask you to try one of these suggestions for a month or two. The time is going to pass anyway, and if you have writer's block already, there's a chance you're going to be in the same predicament as you are now, stuck and no way to escape.

Just take 15-30 minutes of your writing time, or less if you don't even have that much time allotted, and learn a simple meditative exercise or locate an audio program that you like. You don't have anything to loose really except the roadblocks to enjoyable writing. The choice is yours.

BEFORE YOU GO...

I wanted to thank you so very much for purchasing this book. If you enjoyed it and found it helpful, please do me a favor. Before you go, please go back to my sales page and leave a review. Reviews are how other people determine if a book is worth their time and money to purchase and read. Plus, more reviews allow the book to become more visible.

The more reviews this book gets, the more people it can help. If you want to keep up with what I'm up to, visit me on Facebook at:

https://www.facebook.com/WhatThePublishing

or my website and blog at:

http://www.whatthepublishing.com/

If you have any questions or comments, email me at chadkunego@gmail.com and I'll try to respond to them as quickly as I can.

Thank you again for downloading this book and have an awesome day!

APPENDIX A

MY EXPERIENCE WITH MEDITATION AND REDUCED AMOUNTS OF SLEEP

In chapter 2, I talked about being able to function on a reduced amount of sleep and still being productive. Now I'll point out again here that everyone's different, so your results may vary.

For starters, I prefer to get at least 5 hours of sleep a night. I know that I'm not usual in this respect and that most people require more. Don't get me wrong, if left to my own devices, I'd like to sleep 10+ hours if I could. But on a day to day basis, assuming I can't catch a cat nap sometime during the day, I can function indefinitely on 5 hours of sleep a night.

My current amount of sleep is in the 6-7 hour range on a regular basis. If need be, I can function on 4 hours of uninterrupted sleep as long as I can take an hour nap in the afternoon. If I don't get to take that nap, I can keep that schedule for about 3 days before I start to need more sleep. If I can get the nap, I can pretty much do that schedule 5 days a week and catch up on the weekend.

The reason I'm going into this is to allow me to put into perspective what I was able to do for a year straight when I meditated on a daily basis.

About eight years ago I was let go from my main job. At the time, I had a second, part time job which I had to switch to full time. After some searching, I was able to get a second full time job as well. Through the use my preferred standing meditation, I was able to survive on about 2 1/2 hours of uninterrupted sleep and a couple half hour naps in the driver seat of my truck for that full year.

Yes, I was grumpy (some might say downright evil) and no fun to be around, but I was able to stay mentally alert (did tech support for internet, TV, and phone service) and got in great physical shape (I exercised for about 15 min a day with kettlebells before going to sleep and did calisthenics on my breaks throughout the day and between jobs).

Think of it this way, imagine having a newborn baby that stayed a newborn for a full year. I was getting less sleep than that for a full year. I honestly don't think I could have done it without doing my daily meditation.

Would I recommend someone try it…? Absolutely not. If I had to do it again, I would most certainly take up daily meditation and a more intensive exercise program again. I'm just glad that, at this point in my life, I don't have to.

APPENDIX B

BIBLIOGRAPHY/REFERENCES/FURTHER READING

The following is a list of books that I used as reference for this book. They also provide a good basis for further study. Most of these are printed books, but some are available on Kindle as well.

- Bavister, Steve, and Amanda Vickers. *Essential NLP.* Teach Yourself, 2010.

- Buzan, Tony, and Barry Buzan. *The Mind Map Book.* Plume, 1996.

- Harris, Bill. *Thresholds of the Mind.* Centerpoint Press, 2007.

- Heath, Terry. *Write an eBook in 14 Days.* 2013.

- LeShan, Lawrence. *How to Meditate.* Bantam Books, 1974.

- Low, Dene. *Write Like Your Brain Works.* Laurel Wreath Publishing, 2013

- Ostrander, Sheila, and Lynn Schroeder. *Superlearning: Have a supermemory! Improve business and sports performance! Learn anything two to ten times faster!* Laurel, 1979.

- Silva, José, and Philip Miele. *The Silva Mind Control Method.* Pocket Books, 1977.

- Wenger, Win, and Richard Poe. *The Einstein Factor.* Prima, 1996.

NOTES

NOTES

NOTES

www.ingramcontent.com/pod-product-compliance
Lightning Source LLC
Chambersburg PA
CBHW050550280326
41933CB00011B/1784